Aunt Elm & Uncle Poc

A book by RL Lane

Dedicated to an ant…aunt and an ankle…uncle.

"I couldn't figure out where the tree belonged and then I knew once I started Aunt Elm & Uncle Poc…" RL Lane

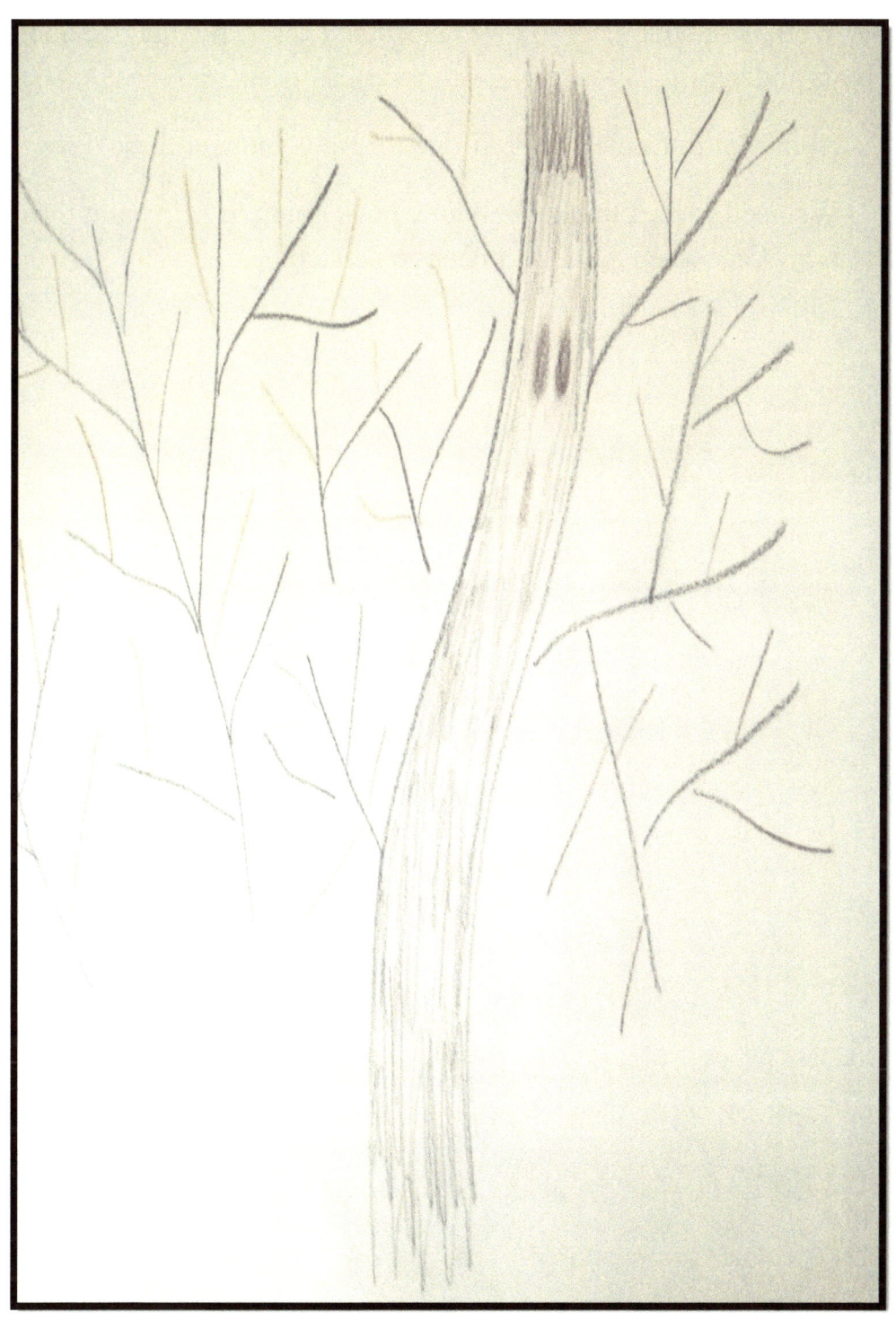

Well, it's about that time we have "the chat"…not the one about the birds and bees…

Aunt Elm & Uncle Poc aren't getting any younger these days…

We need to start thinking about who is going to help paint those walls every year when Aunt Elm needs a new color…

Oh. I forgot to introduce them. Who are they?

Well, Aunt Elm is not a tree…

She is anAuntaMomaWifeaSisteraFriend

Plus she is a professional…she has a job

She works real hard

She is real pretty

She likes to talk a lot

She knows a lot of things

So that makes her talk a lot

She is really creative

She can make anything out of anything

She likes her house…her home

She has a lot of pride

In what her home is like.

Uncle Poc, well he is a man

A tall man

I think he's a little shorter now

He can still grill up those fish

I don't think he catches them anymore

He is a Dad

I think he is more creative after living all those years with Aunt Elm

He is a good friend

He is a really good listener

Which is good because Aunt Elm likes to talk

He would help anyone anytime

How much more do you need to say?

Meet…

Aunt Elm & Uncle Poc

Now they don't really look like this, but this is what my brain drew. Aunt Elm and Uncle Poc have been together for a long time, so maybe Aunt Elm looks like this when she gets mad at Uncle Poc…

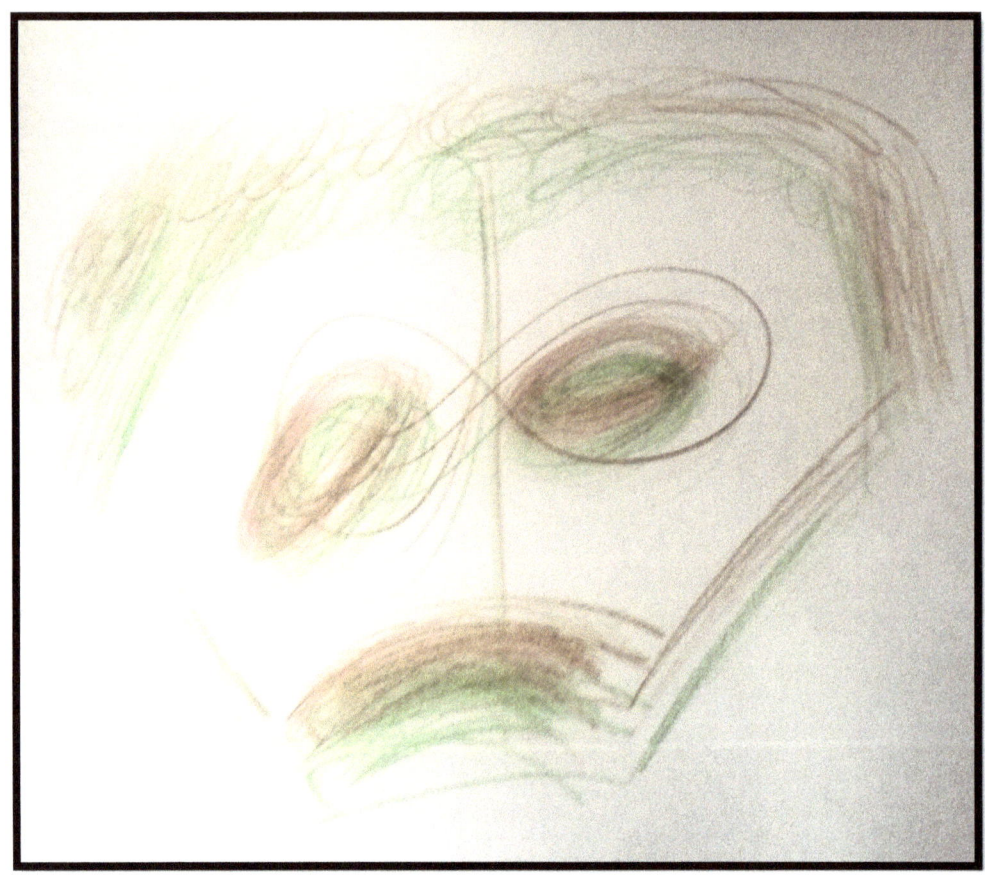

Uncle Poc does get himself into trouble every now and then. He likes to spend time with his friends instead of help with the chores. But, it is true she could always count on Uncle Poc to chase away the riff raff who wanted to befriend their daughters…

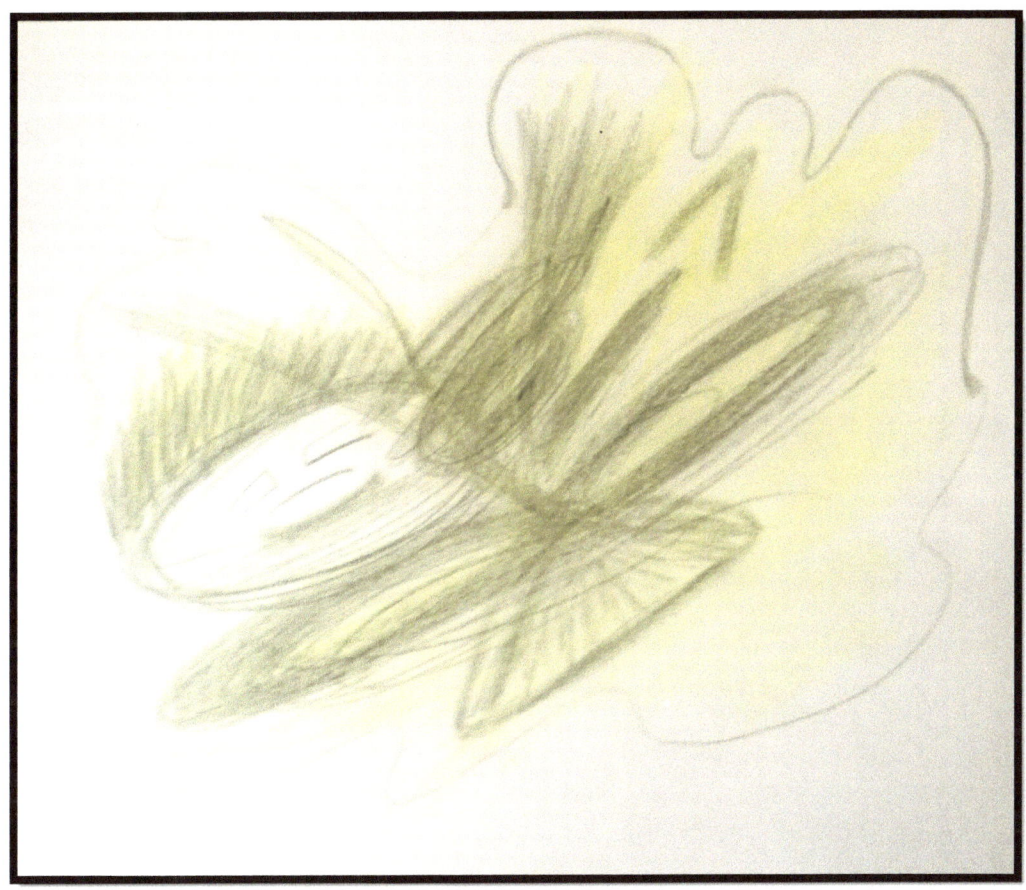

Their house is always in a whirl…it is mostly, like I said, because Aunt Elm likes to change the colors of the walls but it used to be because of all the friends the girls brought home…

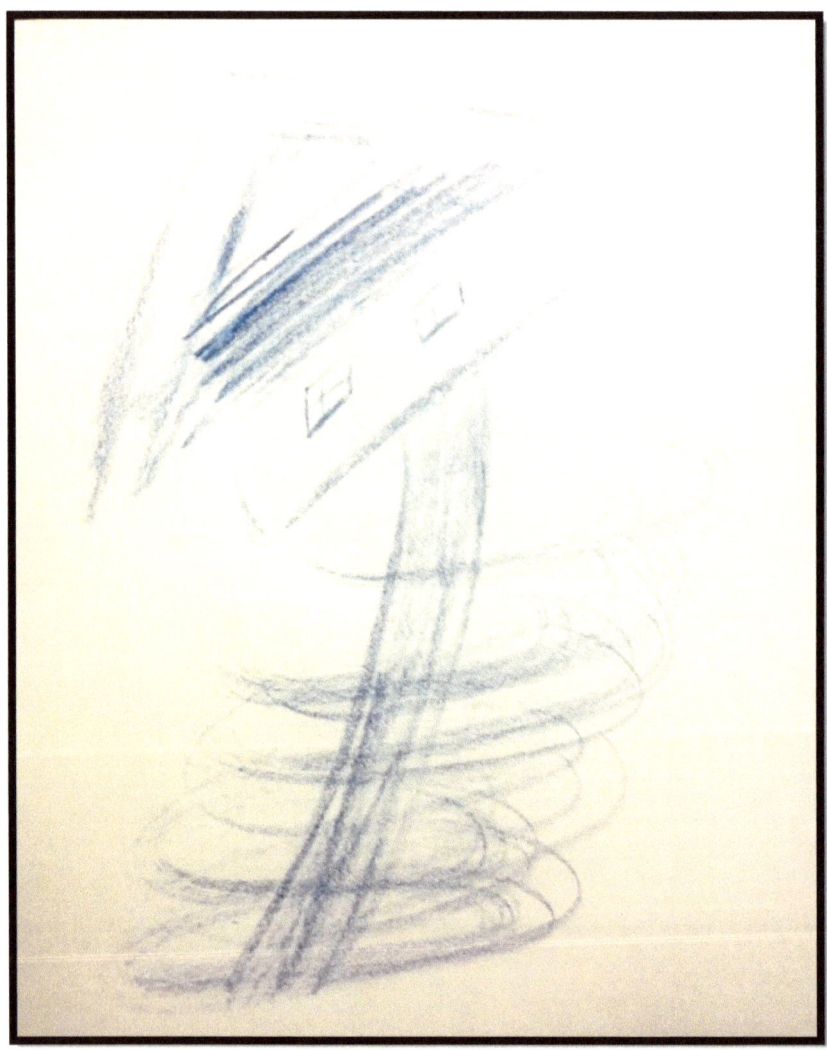

They came to Bhigy Lane because their house was always fun. It probably resembled a circus…

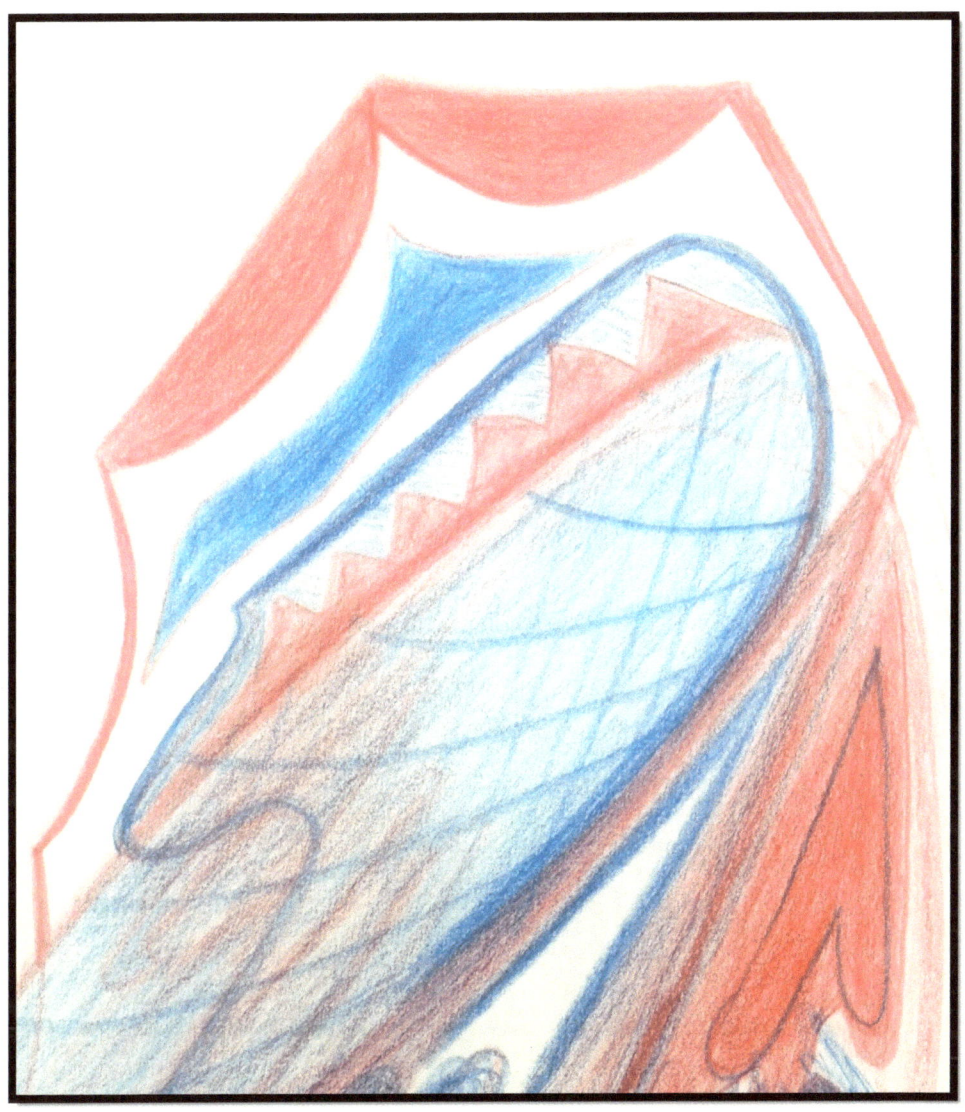

The doors were probably always opening and closing with all those kids coming in and out…and the pets too…

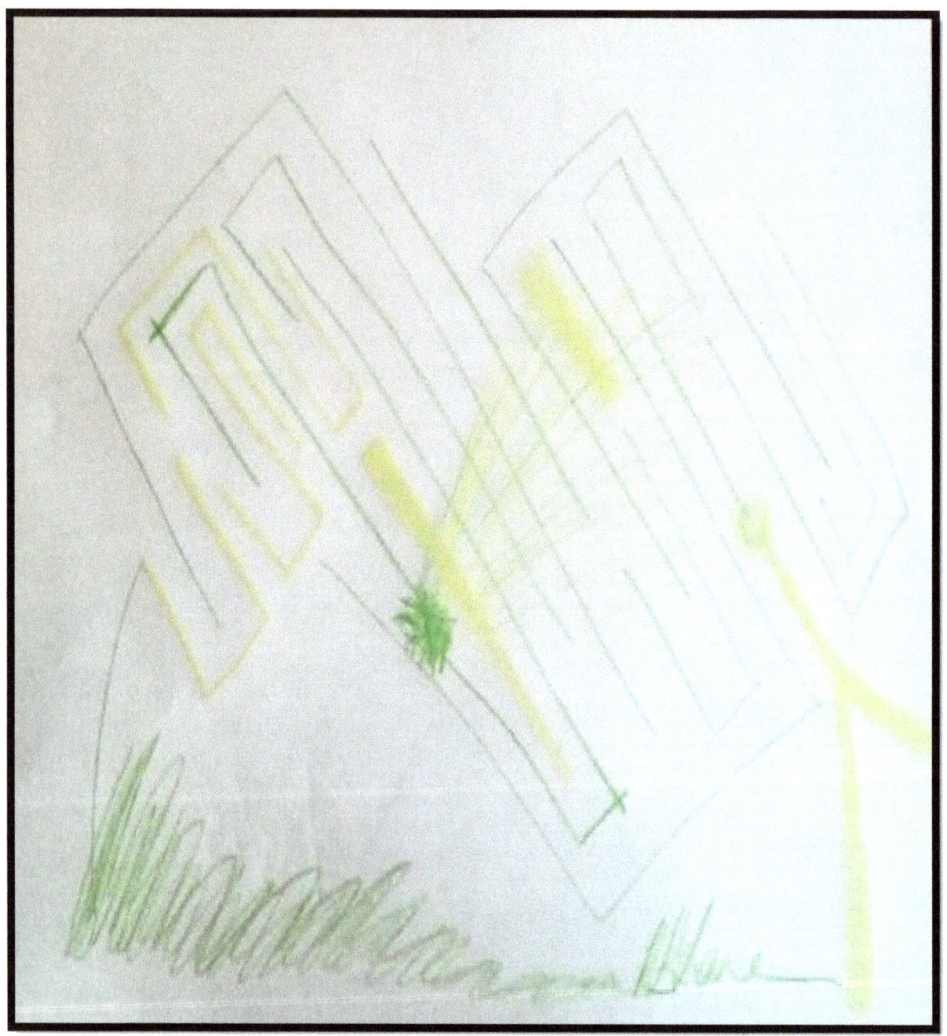

Aunt Elm can make all sorts of special treats. The kind you eat and the kind you get as gifts. Wax dipped pine cones and little doll dresses are on the long list of things she can make. If you ever saw Uncle Poc holding a hanger with wax dipped pinecones you would know he liked Aunt Elm's creations as much as the rest of us.

I often wonder how does she do it all? I don't think Aunt Elm got much sleep in the early years when the girls were growing up. Maybe she really did look like that by the end of those long days. Uncle Poc has glasses and contacts too, but I don't think he wears either one most of the time so he probably didn't really notice if Aunt Elm had a hair or two out of place.

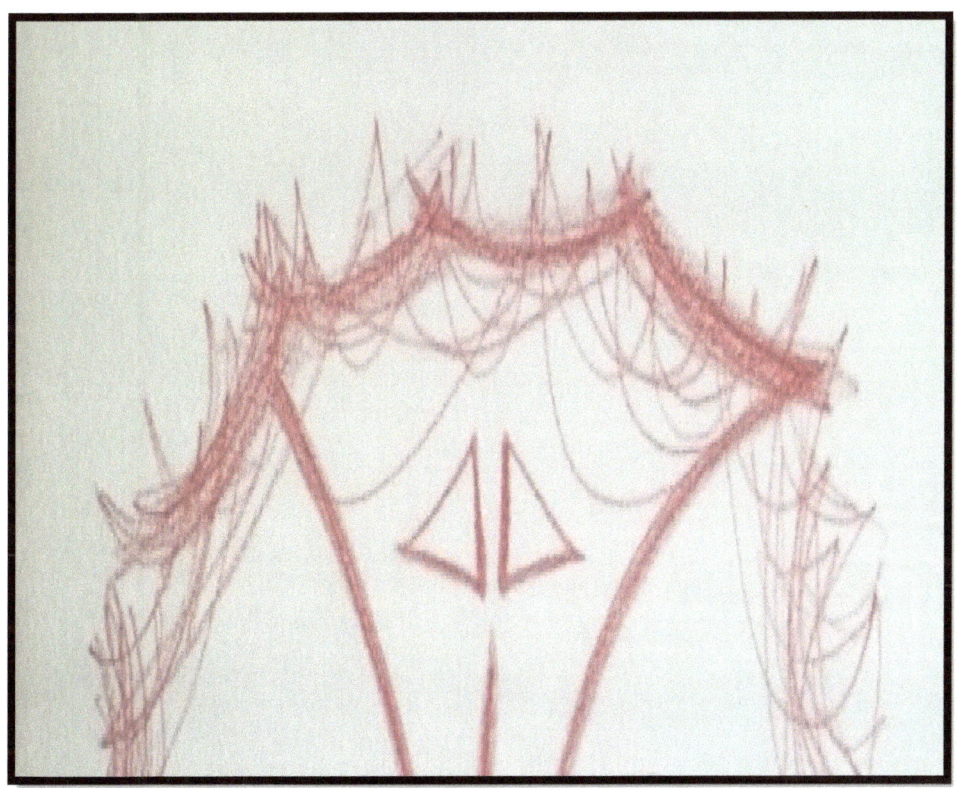

Their story is the story of a lot of Moms and Dads and the years it takes to help their children get on their own two feet…

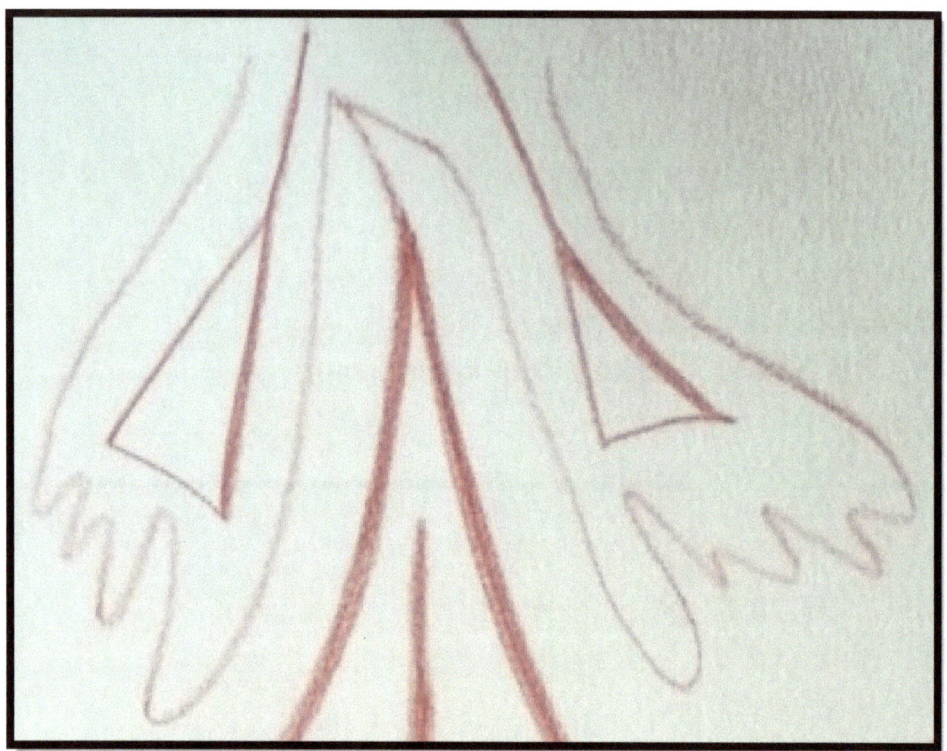

They probably dream of a beach somewhere, resting on the sand, reading books and catching fish…

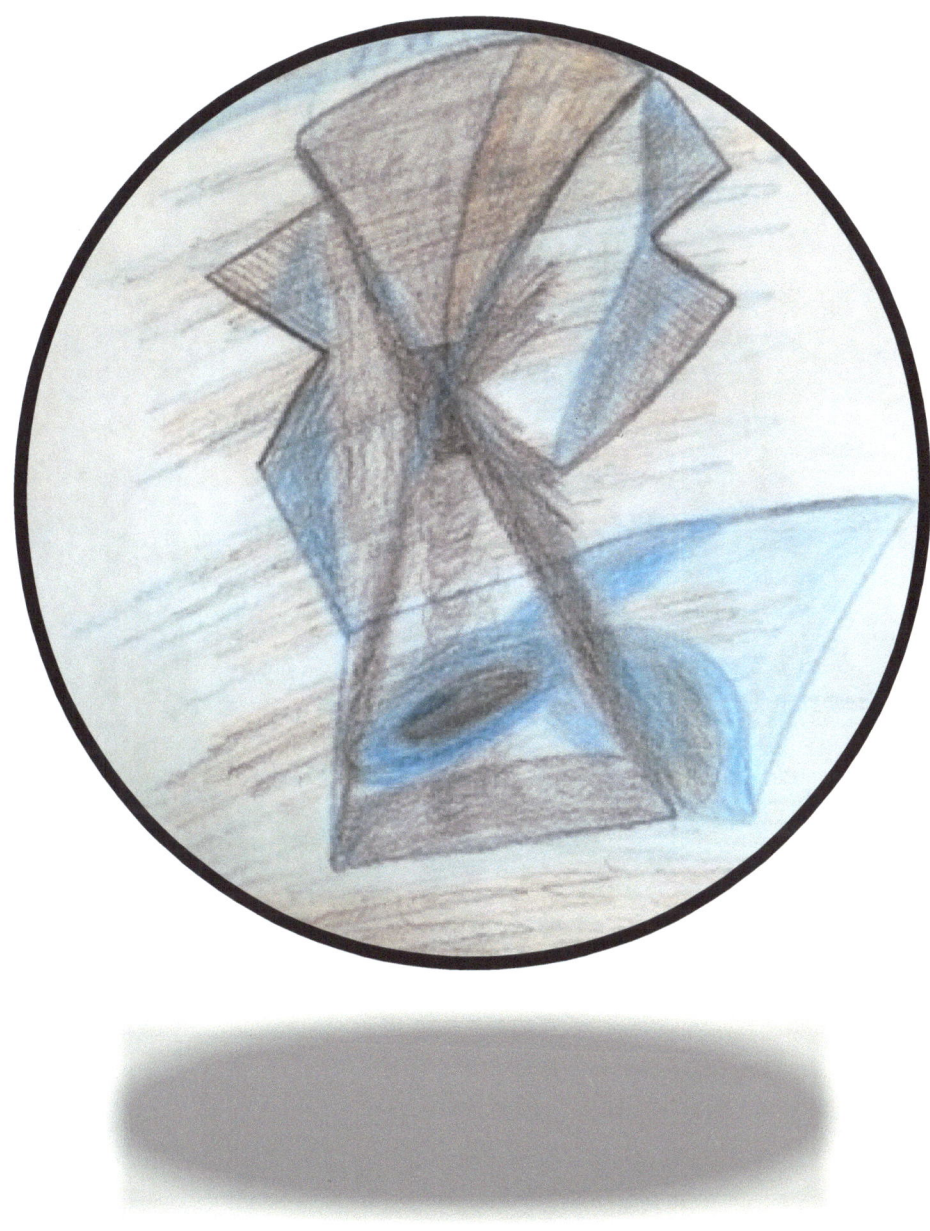

I doubt they want to work for the rest of their days. The thought of that probably makes them want to cry…

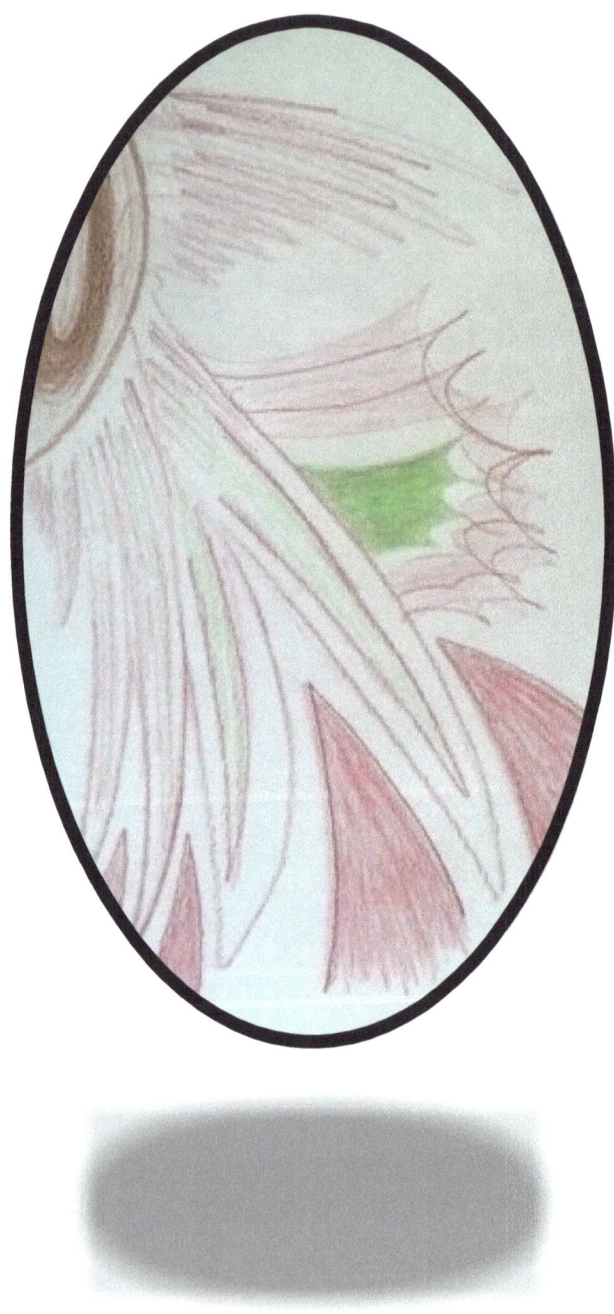

Their house has these sayings on the walls…

The ones Aunt Elm likes to paint.

They are sayings about love and laughter and family…

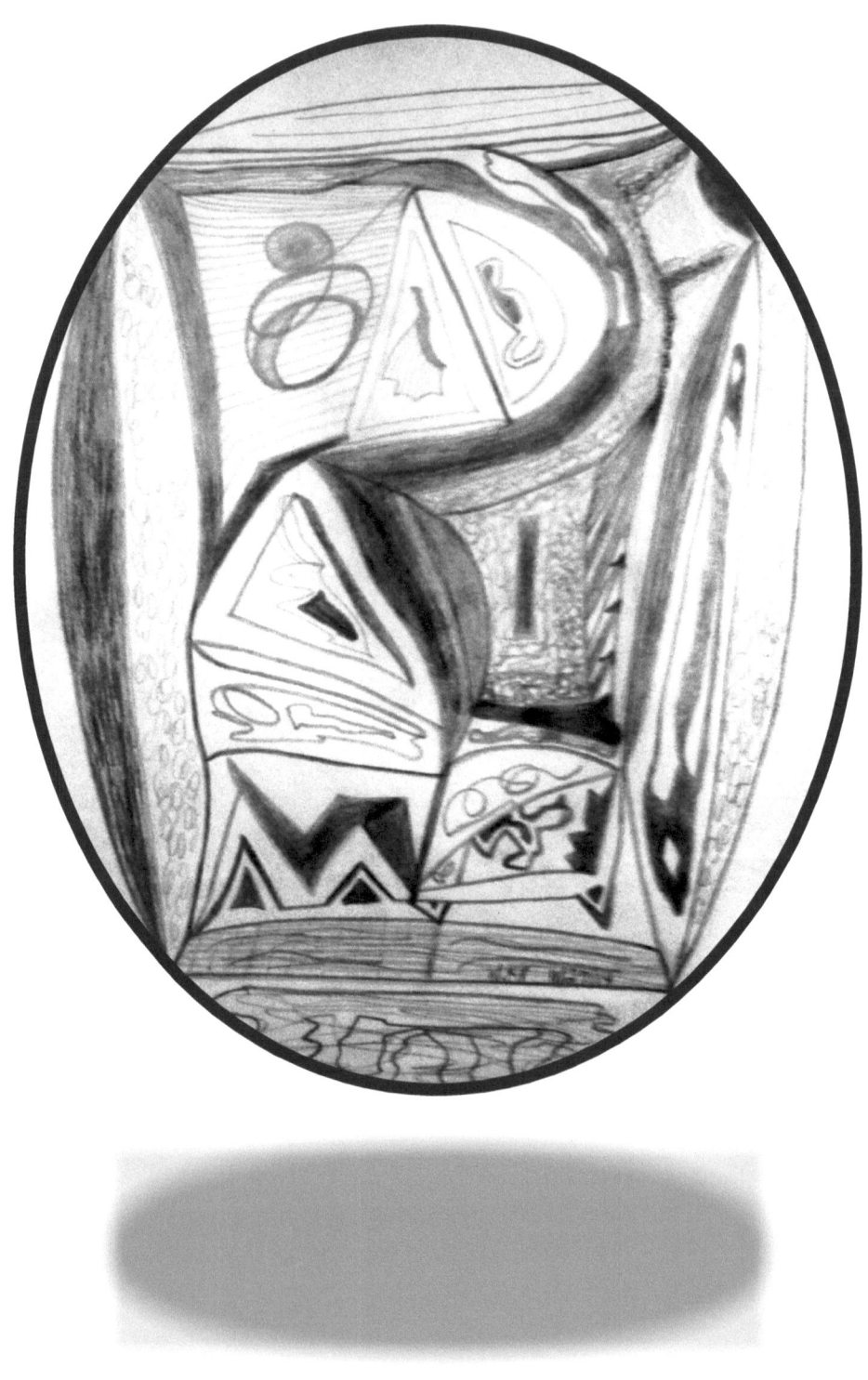

"Family"

Those words remain

Even after the color of the walls have been changed.

It is so they can remember

When their house is quiet and still…

The days of the past and what they really meant…

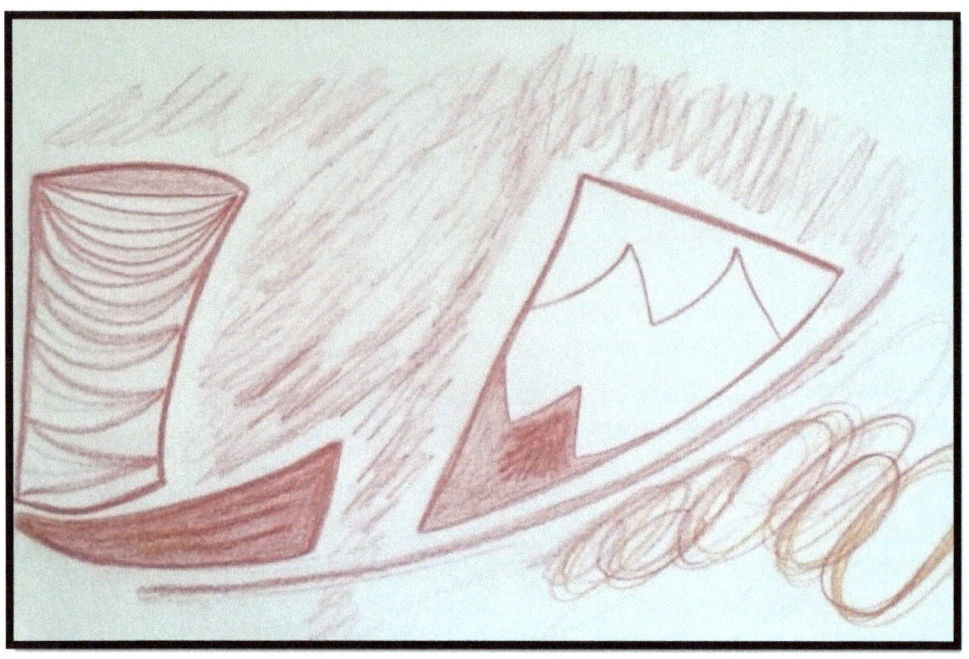

About the Author

RL Lane has published the EcarreT series and a collection of art books featuring the illustrations throughout the books. The series begins with "Chapel Street Signs"...

...unexplained connections that challenge us to beli ve. A woman, a Dad a Doctor, a cat and mouse, a horse and tale tell their stories. "Do you beli ve in spirits?" I asked my friend. "Well look", he said, "I believe there are things that cannot be explained..." Oh. Plus, hear ov a Mom's battle with her struggle to connect to the woman...her little girl.

Welcome to EcarreT...a world
Where everyone cares
Why did I have to create it in...

A fiction fantasy world?

You may already know why, but you will see regardless of what you believe as a girl's journey of love and faith on her "Touring Machine" take her on the best journey of her mundane life. A life well on its way takes a turn in a direction that could've never been seen or even dreamed...

The author can be contacted at:

RosaLeeeLane@gmail.com
www.Amazon.com/author/readrllane

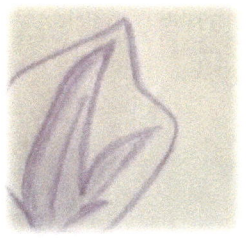

www.ingramcontent.com/pod-product-compliance
Lightning Source LLC
Chambersburg PA
CBHW050432180526
45159CB00006B/2510